the Bo...
HANDBOOK

JOIN OUR FACEBOOK GROUP FOR STORIES, TIPS, TRICKS, WILD CAMPING, BOTHIES AND MORE

WILD CAMPING 101

https://www.facebook.com/groups/474823319998011/

THIS BOOK BELONGS TO

_____

Bothy Name: _____

Date: _____

Time: _____

Grid Reference: _____

OS Map Used: _____

Location: _____

Rating: ☆☆☆☆☆

What sticks out most about this bothy?

_____

_____

_____

Diary, Notes and Experiences.

_____

_____

_____

_____

_____

_____

_____

_____

_____

_____

_____

_____

_____

_____

_____

_____

Draw or Photographs.

Bothy Name: _____

Date: _____

Time: _____

Grid Reference: _____

OS Map Used: _____

Location: _____

Rating: ☆☆☆☆☆

What sticks out most about this bothy?

_____

_____

_____

Diary, Notes and Experiences.

_____

_____

_____

_____

_____

_____

_____

_____

_____

_____

_____

_____

_____

_____

_____

_____

_____

_____

Draw or Photographs.

Bothy Name: _____

Date: _____

Time: _____

Grid Reference: _____

OS Map Used: _____

Location: _____

Rating: ☆☆☆☆☆

What sticks out most about this bothy?

_____

_____

_____

Diary, Notes and Experiences.

_____

_____

_____

_____

_____

_____

_____

_____

_____

_____

_____

_____

_____

_____

_____

_____

Draw or Photographs.

Bothy Name: _____

Date: _____

Time: _____

Grid Reference: _____

OS Map Used: _____

Location: _____

Rating: ☆☆☆☆☆

What sticks out most about this bothy?

_____

_____

_____

Diary, Notes and Experiences.

_____

_____

_____

_____

_____

_____

_____

_____

_____

_____

_____

_____

_____

_____

_____

_____

Draw or Photographs.

Bothy Name: _____

Date: _____

Time: _____

Grid Reference: _____

OS Map Used: _____

Location: _____

Rating: ☆☆☆☆☆

What sticks out most about this bothy?

_____

_____

_____

Diary, Notes and Experiences.

_____

_____

_____

_____

_____

_____

_____

_____

_____

_____

_____

_____

_____

_____

_____

_____

_____

_____

_____

Draw or Photographs.

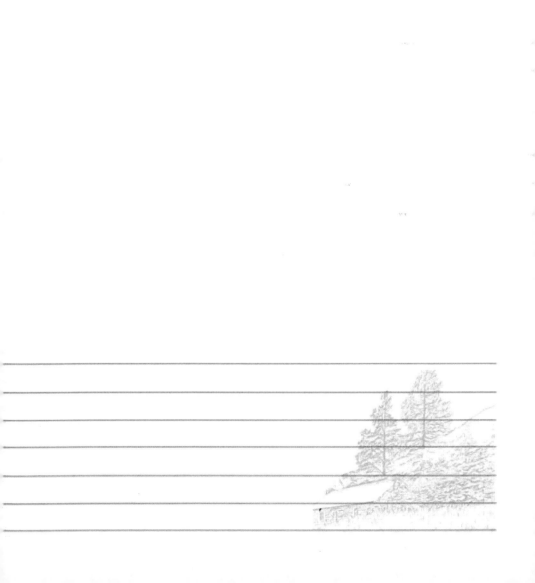

Bothy Name: _____

Date: _____

Time: _____

Grid Reference: _____

OS Map Used: _____

Location: _____

Rating: ☆☆☆☆☆

What sticks out most about this bothy?

_____

_____

_____

Diary, Notes and Experiences.

_____

_____

_____

_____

_____

_____

_____

_____

_____

_____

_____

_____

_____

_____

_____

_____

Draw or Photographs.

Bothy Name: _____

Date: _____

Time: _____

Grid Reference: _____

OS Map Used: _____

Location: _____

Rating: ☆☆☆☆☆

What sticks out most about this bothy?

_____

_____

_____

Diary, Notes and Experiences.

_____

_____

_____

_____

_____

_____

_____

_____

_____

_____

_____

_____

_____

_____

_____

Draw or Photographs.

Bothy Name: _____

Date: _____

Time: _____

Grid Reference: _____

OS Map Used: _____

Location: _____

Rating: ☆☆☆☆☆

What sticks out most about this bothy?

_____

_____

_____

Diary, Notes and Experiences.

_____

_____

_____

_____

_____

_____

_____

_____

_____

_____

_____

_____

_____

_____

Draw or Photographs.

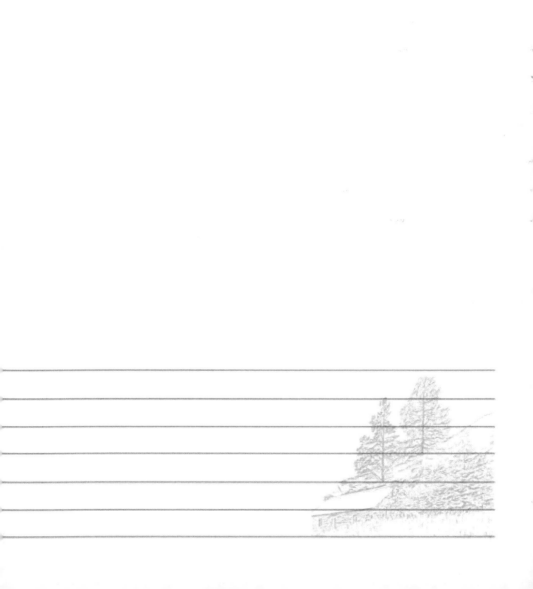

Bothy Name: _____

Date: _____

Time: _____

Grid Reference: _____

OS Map Used: _____

Location: _____

Rating: ☆☆☆☆☆

What sticks out most about this bothy?

_____

_____

_____

Diary, Notes and Experiences.

_____

_____

_____

_____

_____

_____

_____

_____

_____

_____

_____

_____

_____

_____

_____

_____

Draw or Photographs.

Bothy Name: _____

Date: _____

Time: _____

Grid Reference: _____

OS Map Used: _____

Location: _____

Rating: ☆☆☆☆☆

What sticks out most about this bothy?

_____

_____

_____

Diary, Notes and Experiences.

_____

_____

_____

_____

_____

_____

_____

_____

_____

_____

_____

_____

_____

_____

_____

_____

Draw or Photographs.

Bothy Name: _____

Date: _____

Time: _____

Grid Reference: _____

OS Map Used: _____

Location: _____

Rating: ☆☆☆☆☆

What sticks out most about this bothy?

_____

_____

_____

Diary, Notes and Experiences.

_____

_____

_____

_____

_____

_____

_____

_____

_____

_____

_____

_____

_____

_____

_____

_____

_____

Draw or Photographs.

Bothy Name: _____

Date: _____

Time: _____

Grid Reference: _____

OS Map Used: _____

Location: _____

Rating: ☆☆☆☆☆

What sticks out most about this bothy?

_____

_____

_____

Diary, Notes and Experiences.

_____

_____

_____

_____

_____

_____

_____

_____

_____

_____

_____

_____

_____

_____

_____

_____

_____

Draw or Photographs.

Bothy Name: _____

Date: _____

Time: _____

Grid Reference: _____

OS Map Used: _____

Location: _____

Rating: ☆☆☆☆☆

What sticks out most about this bothy?

_____

_____

_____

Diary, Notes and Experiences.

_____

_____

_____

_____

_____

_____

_____

_____

_____

_____

_____

_____

_____

_____

_____

_____

Draw or Photographs.

Bothy Name: _____

Date: _____

Time: _____

Grid Reference: _____

OS Map Used: _____

Location: _____

Rating: ☆☆☆☆☆

What sticks out most about this bothy?

_____

_____

_____

Diary, Notes and Experiences.

_____

_____

_____

_____

_____

_____

_____

_____

_____

_____

_____

_____

_____

_____

_____

_____

Draw or Photographs.

Bothy Name: _____

Date: _____

Time: _____

Grid Reference: _____

OS Map Used: _____

Location: _____

Rating: ☆☆☆☆☆

What sticks out most about this bothy?

_____

_____

_____

Diary, Notes and Experiences.

_____

_____

_____

_____

_____

_____

_____

_____

_____

_____

_____

_____

_____

_____

_____

_____

Draw or Photographs.

Bothy Name: _____

Date: _____

Time: _____

Grid Reference: _____

OS Map Used: _____

Location: _____

Rating: ☆☆☆☆☆

What sticks out most about this bothy?

_____

_____

_____

Diary, Notes and Experiences.

_____

_____

_____

_____

_____

_____

_____

_____

_____

_____

_____

_____

_____

_____

Draw or Photographs.

Bothy Name: _____

Date: _____

Time: _____

Grid Reference: _____

OS Map Used: _____

Location: _____

Rating: ☆☆☆☆☆

What sticks out most about this bothy?

_____
_____
_____

Diary, Notes and Experiences.

_____
_____
_____
_____
_____
_____
_____
_____
_____
_____
_____
_____
_____
_____
_____
_____

Draw or Photographs.

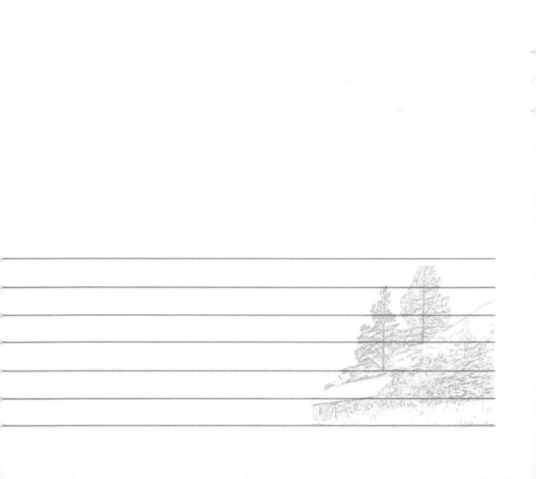

Bothy Name: _____

Date: _____

Time: _____

Grid Reference: _____

OS Map Used: _____

Location: _____

Rating: ☆ ☆ ☆ ☆ ☆

What sticks out most about this bothy?

_____

_____

_____

Diary, Notes and Experiences.

_____

_____

_____

_____

_____

_____

_____

_____

_____

_____

_____

_____

_____

_____

_____

Draw or Photographs.

Bothy Name: _____

Date: _____

Time: _____

Grid Reference: _____

OS Map Used: _____

Location: _____

Rating: ☆☆☆☆☆

What sticks out most about this bothy?

_____

_____

_____

Diary, Notes and Experiences.

_____

_____

_____

_____

_____

_____

_____

_____

_____

_____

_____

_____

_____

_____

_____

_____

_____

Draw or Photographs.

Bothy Name: _____

Date: _____

Time: _____

Grid Reference: _____

OS Map Used: _____

Location: _____

Rating: ☆☆☆☆☆

What sticks out most about this bothy?

_____

_____

_____

Diary, Notes and Experiences.

_____

_____

_____

_____

_____

_____

_____

_____

_____

_____

_____

_____

_____

_____

_____

_____

_____

_____

Draw or Photographs.

Bothy Name: _____

Date: _____

Time: _____

Grid Reference: _____

OS Map Used: _____

Location: _____

Rating: ☆☆☆☆☆

What sticks out most about this bothy?

_____

_____

_____

Diary, Notes and Experiences.

_____

_____

_____

_____

_____

_____

_____

_____

_____

_____

_____

_____

_____

_____

_____

_____

_____

Draw or Photographs.

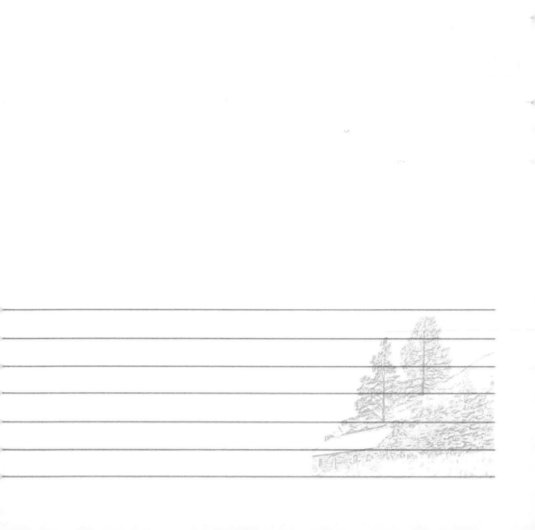

Bothy Name: _____

Date: _____

Time: _____

Grid Reference: _____

OS Map Used: _____

Location: _____

Rating: ☆☆☆☆☆

What sticks out most about this bothy?

_____

_____

_____

Diary, Notes and Experiences.

_____

_____

_____

_____

_____

_____

_____

_____

_____

_____

_____

_____

_____

_____

_____

_____

_____

Draw or Photographs.

Bothy Name: _____

Date: _____

Time: _____

Grid Reference: _____

OS Map Used: _____

Location: _____

Rating: ☆☆☆☆☆

What sticks out most about this bothy?

_____

_____

_____

Diary, Notes and Experiences.

_____

_____

_____

_____

_____

_____

_____

_____

_____

_____

_____

_____

_____

_____

_____

_____

Draw or Photographs.

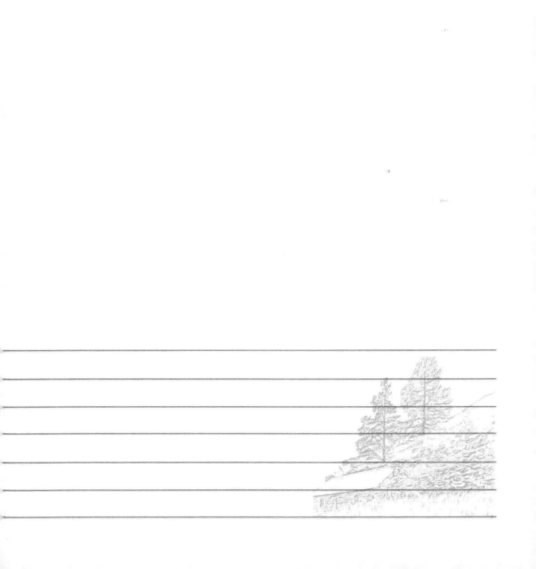

Bothy Name: _____

Date: _____

Time: _____

Grid Reference: _____

OS Map Used: _____

Location: _____

Rating: ☆☆☆☆☆

What sticks out most about this bothy?

_____
_____
_____

Diary, Notes and Experiences.

_____
_____
_____
_____
_____
_____
_____
_____
_____
_____
_____
_____
_____
_____
_____
_____
_____

Draw or Photographs.

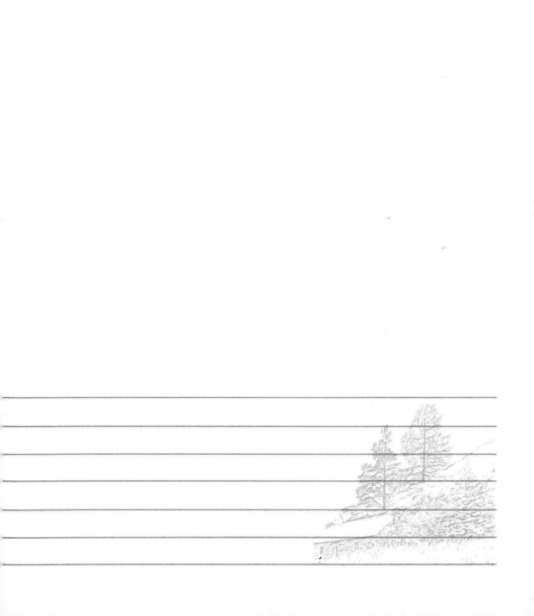

Bothy Name: _____

Date: _____

Time: _____

Grid Reference: _____

OS Map Used: _____

Location: _____

Rating: ☆☆☆☆☆

What sticks out most about this bothy?

_____

_____

_____

Diary, Notes and Experiences.

_____

_____

_____

_____

_____

_____

_____

_____

_____

_____

_____

_____

_____

_____

_____

_____

_____

Draw or Photographs.

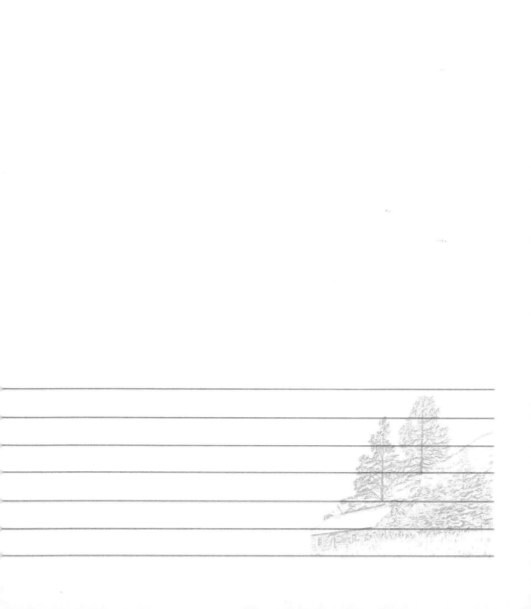

Bothy Name: _____

Date: _____

Time: _____

Grid Reference: _____

OS Map Used: _____

Location: _____

Rating: ☆☆☆☆☆

What sticks out most about this bothy?

_____
_____
_____

Diary, Notes and Experiences.

_____
_____
_____
_____
_____
_____
_____
_____
_____
_____
_____
_____
_____
_____
_____
_____
_____

Draw or Photographs.

Bothy Name: _____

Date: _____

Time: _____

Grid Reference: _____

OS Map Used: _____

Location: _____

Rating: ☆☆☆☆☆

What sticks out most about this bothy?

_____

_____

_____

Diary, Notes and Experiences.

_____

_____

_____

_____

_____

_____

_____

_____

_____

_____

_____

_____

_____

_____

_____

_____

Draw or Photographs.

Bothy Name: _____

Date: _____

Time: _____

Grid Reference: _____

OS Map Used: _____

Location: _____

Rating: ☆☆☆☆☆

What sticks out most about this bothy?

_____

_____

_____

Diary, Notes and Experiences.

_____

_____

_____

_____

_____

_____

_____

_____

_____

_____

_____

_____

_____

_____

_____

Draw or Photographs.

Bothy Name: _____

Date: _____

Time: _____

Grid Reference: _____

OS Map Used: _____

Location: _____

Rating: ☆☆☆☆☆

What sticks out most about this bothy?

_____

_____

_____

Diary, Notes and Experiences.

_____

_____

_____

_____

_____

_____

_____

_____

_____

_____

_____

_____

_____

_____

_____

_____

_____

Draw or Photographs.

Bothy Name: _____

Date: _____

Time: _____

Grid Reference: _____

OS Map Used: _____

Location: _____

Rating: ☆☆☆☆☆

What sticks out most about this bothy?

_____

_____

_____

Diary, Notes and Experiences.

_____

_____

_____

_____

_____

_____

_____

_____

_____

_____

_____

_____

_____

_____

_____

_____

_____

Draw or Photographs.

Bothy Name: _____

Date: _____

Time: _____

Grid Reference: _____

OS Map Used: _____

Location: _____

Rating: ☆☆☆☆☆

What sticks out most about this bothy?

_____

_____

_____

Diary, Notes and Experiences.

_____

_____

_____

_____

_____

_____

_____

_____

_____

_____

_____

_____

_____

_____

_____

_____

Draw or Photographs.

Bothy Name: _____

Date: _____

Time: _____

Grid Reference: _____

OS Map Used: _____

Location: _____

Rating: ☆☆☆☆☆

What sticks out most about this bothy?

_____

_____

_____

Diary, Notes and Experiences.

_____

_____

_____

_____

_____

_____

_____

_____

_____

_____

_____

_____

_____

_____

_____

_____

_____

_____

Draw or Photographs.

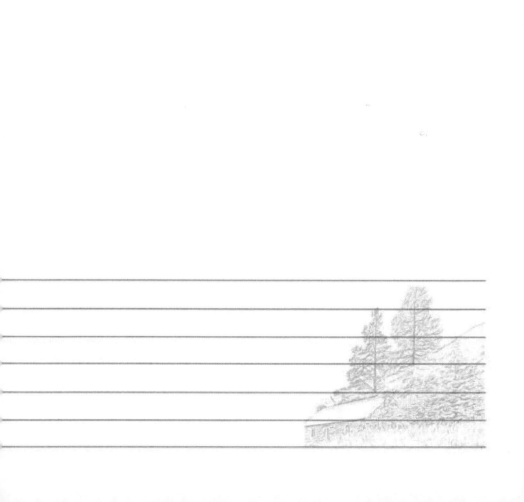

Bothy Name: _____

Date: _____

Time: _____

Grid Reference: _____

OS Map Used: _____

Location: _____

Rating: ☆☆☆☆☆

What sticks out most about this bothy?

_____

_____

_____

Diary, Notes and Experiences.

_____

_____

_____

_____

_____

_____

_____

_____

_____

_____

_____

_____

_____

_____

_____

_____

Draw or Photographs.

Bothy Name: _____

Date: _____

Time: _____

Grid Reference: _____

OS Map Used: _____

Location: _____

Rating: ☆☆☆☆☆

What sticks out most about this bothy?

_____

_____

_____

Diary, Notes and Experiences.

_____

_____

_____

_____

_____

_____

_____

_____

_____

_____

_____

_____

_____

_____

_____

_____

Draw or Photographs.

Bothy Name: _____

Date: _____

Time: _____

Grid Reference: _____

OS Map Used: _____

Location: _____

Rating: ☆☆☆☆☆

What sticks out most about this bothy?

_____

_____

_____

_____

Diary, Notes and Experiences.

_____

_____

_____

_____

_____

_____

_____

_____

_____

_____

_____

_____

_____

_____

_____

_____

_____

Draw or Photographs.

Bothy Name: _____

Date: _____

Time: _____

Grid Reference: _____

OS Map Used: _____

Location: _____

Rating: ☆☆☆☆☆

What sticks out most about this bothy?

_____

_____

_____

Diary, Notes and Experiences.

_____

_____

_____

_____

_____

_____

_____

_____

_____

_____

_____

_____

_____

_____

_____

_____

_____

_____

Draw or Photographs.

Bothy Name: _____

Date: _____

Time: _____

Grid Reference: _____

OS Map Used: _____

Location: _____

Rating: ☆☆☆☆☆

What sticks out most about this bothy?

_____

_____

_____

Diary, Notes and Experiences.

_____

_____

_____

_____

_____

_____

_____

_____

_____

_____

_____

_____

_____

_____

_____

_____

Draw or Photographs.

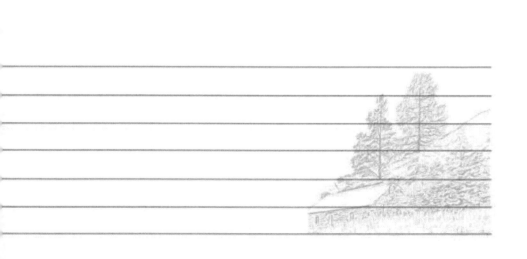

Bothy Name: _____

Date: _____

Time: _____

Grid Reference: _____

OS Map Used: _____

Location: _____

Rating: ☆☆☆☆☆

What sticks out most about this bothy?

_____

_____

_____

Diary, Notes and Experiences.

_____

_____

_____

_____

_____

_____

_____

_____

_____

_____

_____

_____

_____

_____

_____

_____

Draw or Photographs.

Bothy Name: _____

Date: _____

Time: _____

Grid Reference: _____

OS Map Used: _____

Location: _____

Rating: ☆☆☆☆☆

What sticks out most about this bothy?

_____

_____

_____

Diary, Notes and Experiences.

_____

_____

_____

_____

_____

_____

_____

_____

_____

_____

_____

_____

_____

_____

_____

_____

_____

Draw or Photographs.

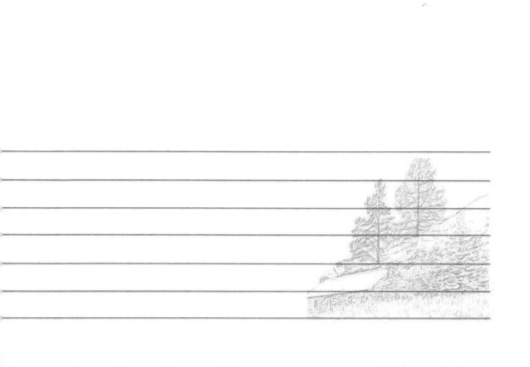

Bothy Name: _____

Date: _____

Time: _____

Grid Reference: _____

OS Map Used: _____

Location: _____

Rating: ☆☆☆☆☆

What sticks out most about this bothy?

_____

_____

_____

Diary, Notes and Experiences.

_____

_____

_____

_____

_____

_____

_____

_____

_____

_____

_____

_____

_____

_____

_____

_____

Draw or Photographs.

Bothy Name: _____

Date: _____

Time: _____

Grid Reference: _____

OS Map Used: _____

Location: _____

Rating: ☆☆☆☆☆

What sticks out most about this bothy?

_____

_____

_____

Diary, Notes and Experiences.

_____

_____

_____

_____

_____

_____

_____

_____

_____

_____

_____

_____

_____

_____

_____

Draw or Photographs.

Bothy Name: _____

Date: _____

Time: _____

Grid Reference: _____

OS Map Used: _____

Location: _____

Rating: ☆☆☆☆☆

What sticks out most about this bothy?

_____

_____

_____

Diary, Notes and Experiences.

_____

_____

_____

_____

_____

_____

_____

_____

_____

_____

_____

_____

_____

_____

_____

_____

_____

Draw or Photographs.

Bothy Name: _____

Date: _____

Time: _____

Grid Reference: _____

OS Map Used: _____

Location: _____

Rating: ☆☆☆☆☆

What sticks out most about this bothy?

_____

_____

_____

Diary, Notes and Experiences.

_____

_____

_____

_____

_____

_____

_____

_____

_____

_____

_____

_____

_____

_____

_____

_____

_____

Draw or Photographs.

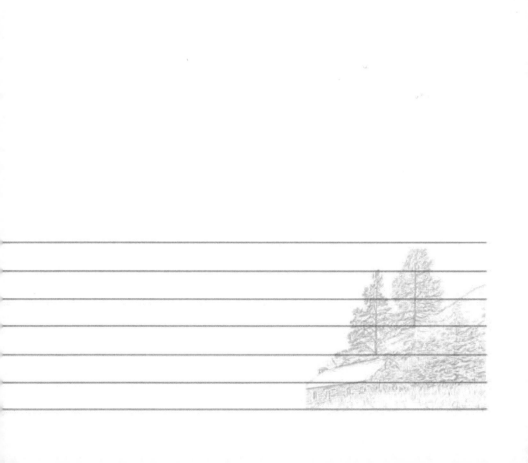

Bothy Name: _____

Date: _____

Time: _____

Grid Reference: _____

OS Map Used: _____

Location: _____

Rating: ☆☆☆☆☆

What sticks out most about this bothy?

_____

_____

_____

Diary, Notes and Experiences.

_____

_____

_____

_____

_____

_____

_____

_____

_____

_____

_____

_____

_____

_____

_____

_____

_____

Draw or Photographs.

Bothy Name: _____

Date: _____

Time: _____

Grid Reference: _____

OS Map Used: _____

Location: _____

Rating: ☆☆☆☆☆

What sticks out most about this bothy?

_____

_____

_____

Diary, Notes and Experiences.

_____

_____

_____

_____

_____

_____

_____

_____

_____

_____

_____

_____

_____

_____

_____

_____

_____

_____

Draw or Photographs.

Bothy Name: _____

Date: _____

Time: _____

Grid Reference: _____

OS Map Used: _____

Location: _____

Rating: ☆☆☆☆☆

What sticks out most about this bothy?

_____

_____

_____

Diary, Notes and Experiences.

_____

_____

_____

_____

_____

_____

_____

_____

_____

_____

_____

_____

_____

_____

_____

_____

_____

_____

Draw or Photographs.

Bothy Name: _____

Date: _____

Time: _____

Grid Reference: _____

OS Map Used: _____

Location: _____

Rating: ☆☆☆☆☆

What sticks out most about this bothy?

_____

_____

_____

Diary, Notes and Experiences.

_____

_____

_____

_____

_____

_____

_____

_____

_____

_____

_____

_____

_____

_____

_____

_____

_____

_____

Draw or Photographs.

Bothy Name: _____

Date: _____

Time: _____

Grid Reference: _____

OS Map Used: _____

Location: _____

Rating: ☆☆☆☆☆

What sticks out most about this bothy?

_____
_____
_____
_____

Diary, Notes and Experiences.

_____
_____
_____
_____
_____
_____
_____
_____
_____
_____
_____
_____
_____
_____
_____
_____
_____
_____

Draw or Photographs.

Bothy Name: _____

Date: _____

Time: _____

Grid Reference: _____

OS Map Used: _____

Location: _____

Rating: ☆☆☆☆☆

What sticks out most about this bothy?

_____

_____

_____

Diary, Notes and Experiences.

_____

_____

_____

_____

_____

_____

_____

_____

_____

_____

_____

_____

_____

_____

_____

_____

_____

_____

Draw or Photographs.

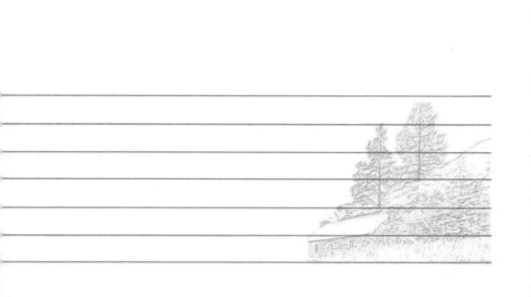

Bothy Name: _____

Date: _____

Time: _____

Grid Reference: _____

OS Map Used: _____

Location: _____

Rating: ☆☆☆☆☆

What sticks out most about this bothy?

_____

_____

_____

Diary, Notes and Experiences.

_____

_____

_____

_____

_____

_____

_____

_____

_____

_____

_____

_____

_____

_____

_____

_____

_____

Draw or Photographs.

Bothy Name: _____

Date: _____

Time: _____

Grid Reference: _____

OS Map Used: _____

Location: _____

Rating: ☆☆☆☆☆

What sticks out most about this bothy?

_____

_____

_____

Diary, Notes and Experiences.

_____

_____

_____

_____

_____

_____

_____

_____

_____

_____

_____

_____

_____

_____

_____

_____

_____

Draw or Photographs.

Bothy Name: _____

Date: _____

Time: _____

Grid Reference: _____

OS Map Used: _____

Location: _____

Rating: ☆☆☆☆☆

What sticks out most about this bothy?

_____

_____

_____

Diary, Notes and Experiences.

_____

_____

_____

_____

_____

_____

_____

_____

_____

_____

_____

_____

_____

_____

_____

_____

_____

Draw or Photographs.

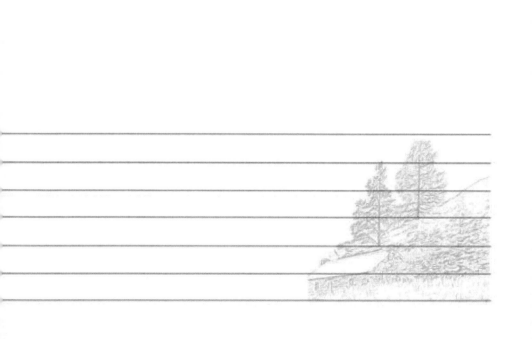

Bothy Name: _____

Date: _____

Time: _____

Grid Reference: _____

OS Map Used: _____

Location: _____

Rating: ☆☆☆☆☆

What sticks out most about this bothy?

_____

_____

_____

Diary, Notes and Experiences.

_____

_____

_____

_____

_____

_____

_____

_____

_____

_____

_____

_____

_____

_____

_____

_____

_____

_____

Draw or Photographs.

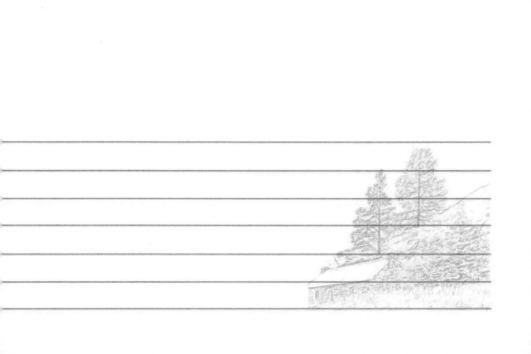

Bothy Name: _____

Date: _____

Time: _____

Grid Reference: _____

OS Map Used: _____

Location: _____

Rating: ☆☆☆☆☆

What sticks out most about this bothy?

_____

_____

_____

Diary, Notes and Experiences.

_____

_____

_____

_____

_____

_____

_____

_____

_____

_____

_____

_____

_____

_____

_____

_____

Draw or Photographs.

Bothy Name: _____

Date: _____

Time: _____

Grid Reference: _____

OS Map Used: _____

Location: _____

Rating: ☆☆☆☆☆

What sticks out most about this bothy?

_____
_____
_____
_____

Diary, Notes and Experiences.

_____
_____
_____
_____
_____
_____
_____
_____
_____
_____
_____
_____
_____
_____
_____
_____
_____
_____
_____

Draw or Photographs.

Bothy Name: _____

Date: _____

Time: _____

Grid Reference: _____

OS Map Used: _____

Location: _____

Rating: ☆☆☆☆☆

What sticks out most about this bothy?

_____

_____

_____

Diary, Notes and Experiences.

_____

_____

_____

_____

_____

_____

_____

_____

_____

_____

_____

_____

_____

_____

_____

_____

_____

Draw or Photographs.

Bothy Name: _____

Date: _____

Time: _____

Grid Reference: _____

OS Map Used: _____

Location: _____

Rating: ☆☆☆☆☆

What sticks out most about this bothy?

_____

_____

_____

Diary, Notes and Experiences.

_____

_____

_____

_____

_____

_____

_____

_____

_____

_____

_____

_____

_____

_____

_____

_____

_____

_____

Draw or Photographs.

Bothy Name: _____

Date: _____

Time: _____

Grid Reference: _____

OS Map Used: _____

Location: _____

Rating: ☆☆☆☆☆

What sticks out most about this bothy?

_____

_____

_____

Diary, Notes and Experiences.

_____

_____

_____

_____

_____

_____

_____

_____

_____

_____

_____

_____

_____

_____

_____

_____

_____

Draw or Photographs.

Bothy Name: _____

Date: _____

Time: _____

Grid Reference: _____

OS Map Used: _____

Location: _____

Rating: ☆☆☆☆☆

What sticks out most about this bothy?

_____

_____

_____

Diary, Notes and Experiences.

_____

_____

_____

_____

_____

_____

_____

_____

_____

_____

_____

_____

_____

_____

_____

_____

_____

Draw or Photographs.

Bothy Name: _____

Date: _____

Time: _____

Grid Reference: _____

OS Map Used: _____

Location: _____

Rating: ☆☆☆☆☆

What sticks out most about this bothy?

_____

_____

_____

Diary, Notes and Experiences.

_____

_____

_____

_____

_____

_____

_____

_____

_____

_____

_____

_____

_____

_____

_____

_____

_____

Draw or Photographs.

Printed in Great Britain
by Amazon